Davenport

WITHDRAWN

Donowler

be a winner in
BASEBALL

By the Same Author

Aerospace Pilot
Aerospace Power, *a Pictorial Guide*
Auto Racing
Bicycling
Bush Flying in Alaska
Cleared for Takeoff, *Behind the Scenes at an Airport*
Deep-Sea World, *the Story of Oceanography*
Drag Racing
Gateway to Space
Lift-Off, *the Story of Rocket Power*
Motorcycling
Project Apollo, *Mission to the Moon*
Project Mercury
Rockets, Missiles, and Moons
Skyhooks, *the Story of Helicopters*
Skylab
Skyrocketing Into the Unknown
Spacetrack, *Watchdog of the Skies*

be a winner in
BASEBALL

CHARLES COOMBS

illustrated with 65 photographs and diagrams
William Morrow and Company
New York 1973

Coombs, Charles Ira, (date)
   Be a winner in baseball.

   SUMMARY: Presents a brief history of baseball and instructs in
improving the basic skills needed to play the game: sliding into base,
fielding ground balls, making judgments, and many others.
   1. Baseball—Juvenile literature.   [1. Baseball]
I. Title.
GV867.5.C66   796.357   72-7744
ISBN 0-688-20062-1
ISBN 0-688-30062-6 (lib. bdg.)

Permission for photographs is gratefully acknowledged: American League
of Professional Baseball Clubs, page 13; Atlanta Braves, pages 43, left,
47, 75, 97, 113, 116; Chicago National League Ball Club (Inc.), pages 62,
63, 77, 102; Chicago White Sox, page 4; Hillerich & Bradsby Co, page 69;
Houston Astros, page 104; Little League Baseball, page 24; Los Angeles
Dodgers, Inc., pages 101, 105; MacGregor, pages 20, 21, 76; Minnesota
Twins, pages 27, 64; Montreal Expos, pages 89, 91; National League,
page 17; Oakland A's, page 88; Philadelphia Phillies, page 98; Pittsburgh
Baseball Club, page 59; The San Diego *Union,* pages 106, 108.

All other photographs were taken by the author.

contents

be a winner in
BASEBALL

first inning

THE GAME

What is the game of baseball?

It is a fellow out in right field loafing, with his hands on his knees, a batter at homeplate rapping the dirt from his cleats, an infield player spitting into his glove, a player wiping sweat from his forehead, then stepping briskly to the pitcher's mound. It is a team of boys or men, or occasionally girls, waiting for something to happen. At last the pitcher rears back and hurls the ball toward a rubber pad, seventeen inches wide and guarded by an opposing player wielding a yard-long chunk of rounded hardwood.

11

Baseball is a ballet of well-timed action.

With that pitch, the game bursts into action. The bat cracks against horsehide, and nine defensive players race, leap, dive, catch, throw, and do whatever else is legally possible to prevent opposing players from reaching any of the bases set at the corners of a diamond-shaped playing field.

That is baseball.

It is a game for everyone. You cannot be too little or too big to play, or too light or too heavy, too fast,

Baseball is a game for everyone.

too slow. Of course, to be a good player, you should have strong arms and legs, decent speed, and quick hands. You should, in fact, keep yourself in top physical condition. But the main thing you need is the desire to play. You must want to play badly enough to be willing to put in the time and effort to get in shape, keep in shape, and learn the many skills of the game.

You must also like to compete. You should have the

urge to win. You must be eager and, most of all, you must use your head. Baseball is as much a thinking game as it is a game of action.

No one really knows just when and where baseball began. Some believe that it developed from the English game of cricket, which was introduced to the American colonies around 1750. Long before the game was even called baseball, informal teams simply got together on a vacant field. They played a hitting and running game that, in time, became a favorite pastime in the United States.

A player used an old cricket bat, a tree branch, an ax handle, or whatever he could swing at a pitched ball. Hitters banged away at thrown balls and tried to reach a stake stuck in the ground before opposing players "plugged" them—that is, hit them with the ball. Years later this harsh method of putting a man out gave way to the more gentle procedure in which a fielder touches the proper base or tags the runner.

In the 1800's the game began to change. For one thing, running at stakes stuck in the ground proved dangerous. A player sometimes tripped and fell on one, or was pushed and injured. Stakes were replaced by flat stones in the early 1830's. But even stones

14

could cut a sliding runner or cause a twisted ankle, so stones gave way to bags filled with sand and anchored in position so they couldn't be pushed around. Before bases were pegged down, a slick infielder might kick the stone out of a runner's reach and tag him out.

Up until 1839, the game remained an informal affair, with few set rules. In that year a man named Abner Doubleday, who lived in Cooperstown, New York, the present site of the National Baseball Hall of Fame, decided that the game was worth standardizing. He gave it the official name of baseball, although many people probably began calling it baseball shortly after stones and sand-filled bases had replaced stakes. From "run to your stake," the shout became "run to your base," and, logically, the name *baseball* emerged.

History remains uncertain concerning just what and how far-reaching were Doubleday's contributions to the game. He often is credited with drawing the first diagram of a diamond-shaped playing field. In any case, what Doubleday started, a New Yorker named Alexander Cartwright finished about 1845. Cartwright laid out the dimensions of the diamond, which have remained virtually the same ever since. He established a distance of ninety feet between bases. The team was

15

composed of nine players, whereas before the number depended on how many fellows showed up on the field.

Not all of Cartwright's rules remained permanent, however. He put the pitcher just forty-five feet from home plate, which proved to be too close for comfort. Later this distance was changed to the present official sixty feet, six inches. Why the six inches? Well, the story is that when the change was made, someone wrote, not very clearly, *60' 0"* on the diagram for the diamond. Whoever laid out the field mistook the *0* for a *6* and placed the pitcher's rubber sixty feet, six inches from the rear tip of home plate. There it remains. And the distance has worked out very well, making possible the endless duels between pitchers and batters. The ninety-foot distance between bases also has proved an ideal distance for the competition between runners and fielders. Whether the ball or the runner reaches base first is often a close play.

Other developments quickly followed. What had formerly been called *hands* came to be called *innings*. And instead of an *ace,* a score was called a *run.* The catcher, who for safety's sake had played far in back of home plate, was moved up directly behind the batter.

Opposite: Official baseball diamond

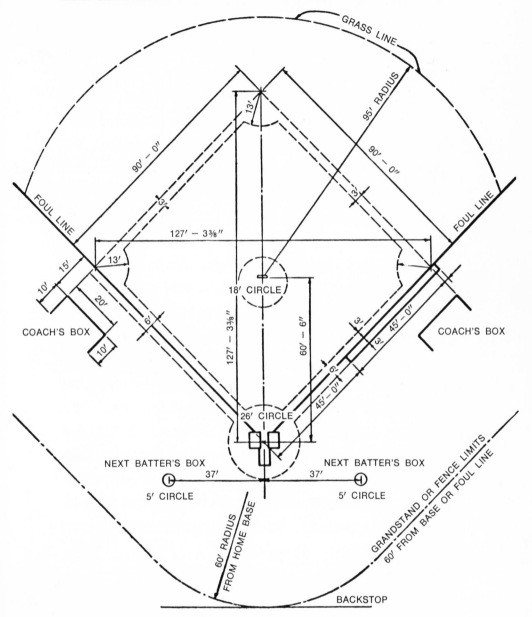

LEGEND

— BASE LINES, BATTER'S BOX, CATCHER'S BOX,
FOUL LINE, PITCHER'S PLATE, COACH'S BOX
○ NEXT BATTER'S BOX
--- BASE LINES
— — GRASS LINES

GRASS LINE

95' RADIUS

90' – 0"

13'

90' – 0"

3'

3'

FOUL LINE

FOUL LINE

127' – 3⅜"

13'

15'

10'

20'

6'

10'

COACH'S BOX

COACH'S BOX

18' CIRCLE

127' – 3⅜"

60' – 6"

3'

3'

45' – 0"

6'

45' – 0"

26' CIRCLE

NEXT BATTER'S BOX

37'

NEXT BATTER'S BOX

37'

5' CIRCLE

5' CIRCLE

GRANDSTAND OR FENCE LIMITS
60' FROM BASE OR FOUL LINE

60' RADIUS
FROM HOME BASE

BACKSTOP

But he began to wear a mask and pads in order to protect himself as well as he could from the battering to which catchers are subject. As yet no one had thought of using gloves or mitts to help catch the ball. That refinement came still later.

The game had been played mostly in the northern United States until the 1860's. During the Civil War, however, Southern soldiers turned to baseball for recreation. It also was played in prison camps.

Following the war, baseball gained rapidly in popularity. In 1869, the Cincinnati Red Stockings became the first all-professional team. The players wore distinctive uniforms, including, of course, red stockings. The Cincinnati catcher, having bruised the palm of his catching hand one day, snipped the fingers off a regular street glove, thereby introducing baseball mitts.

It was around this same time that a Brooklyn pitcher named William (Candy) Cummings accidentally put some extra spin on the ball and threw a curve. Baseball had found a new offensive weapon.

As the game continued to improve, people began paying to see it, and the baseball fan came into being. More professional teams were created. In 1876, the various teams were formed into the National League, still known as the senior circuit of professional baseball. The number of professional teams continued to expand, and in 1900 the American League was organized.

For several years each league played only for its own championship. Then, in 1903, the winning teams of each league challenged one another to a play-off to determine the year's all-around best team. Thus, the World Series was born.

Baseball has changed very little in the past half century or so. Its rules are quite simple. As a player on the offensive team, you stand in the batter's box clutching a rounded hardwood stick. You dig in, determined not to let the pitcher on the opposing team throw a ball in the strike zone past you. In addition to the pitcher, there are eight other players on the defensive team out on the diamond. They are poised to catch the ball you hit, put you out with a base throw, tag you off the base, or do whatever else is necessary to keep you from hitting the ball past them and running safely around the bases to score a run.

In addition to the standard-sized diamond (scaled down for teams of young players such as Little League), other official regulations have come into

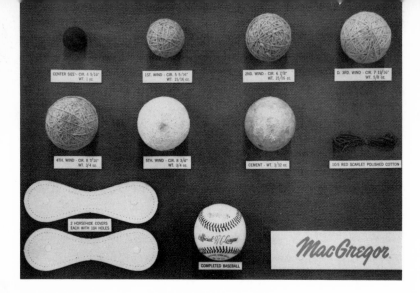

CENTER SIZE - CIR. 4 5/16"
WT. 1 oz.

1ST. WIND - CIR. 5 5/16"
WT. 15/16 oz.

2ND. WIND - CIR. 6 7/8"
WT. 15/16 oz.

D. 3RD. WIND - CIR. 7 13/16"
WT. 5/8 oz.

4TH. WIND - CIR. 8 7/16"
WT. 3/4 oz.

5TH. WIND - CIR. 8 3/4"
WT. 3/4 oz.

CEMENT - WT. 3/32 oz.

10-5 RED SCARLET POLISHED COTTON

2 HORSEHIDE COVERS
EACH WITH 104 HOLES

COMPLETED BASEBALL

MacGregor

The official baseball is ingeniously made from
an assortment of parts carefully assembled.

being. The hard ball is made of a cork and rubber
core, wound by layers of string, and finished off with
a cover of tightly stitched leather. It weighs between
five and five and one-quarter ounces, and it is nine to
nine and one-quarter inches around.

There are restrictions governing the makeup of various fielders' gloves (except for the catcher's mitt).
The mitt or glove should not be more than a foot long
from heel to fingertip, nor more than eight inches wide
across the palm, from thumb crotch to the outer edge
of the glove. There is a rule on the allowable width
and depth of the space between the thumb and the in-

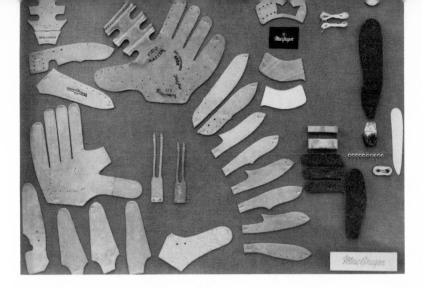

Baseball gloves are designed and engineered to reduce catching errors.

dex finger and another on the type and amount of webbing that may be used to fill that space. These standards prevent players from making a basket of their mitts or gloves and so catching the ball more easily.

Uniforms may not have shiny buttons that can reflect the sun into a player's eyes. The uniform cannot have a patch or other insignia sewed on it that resembles a baseball, which could confuse the eye of an opposing player.

There are other fine points to the game. Each position on the field provides the player with unique problems. Certainly the fellow standing in the batter's box faces all kinds of hurdles set up to keep him from hitting the ball and safely reaching base. And the base runner has the constant challenge of trying to beat the throw of an opposing fielder bent on cutting off his progress toward home plate.

Like snowflakes, which never duplicate themselves, no two baseball games are ever alike. The endless variety makes baseball the great game it is. You can find a place in baseball to fit your particular skills: pitching, catching, batting, running, throwing, or, ideally, a combination of several. It is, indeed, a game that every boy should try, for determination and practice, more than natural talent, really make the ballplayer.

Whoever or wherever you are, "Play ball!"

22

second inning
TRAINING AND PRACTICE

To play good baseball you have to be in top shape both mentally and physically. Furthermore, you never can reach your peak of performance unless you practice, practice, and practice some more.

You may aspire to become a big-league ballplayer. There is really no reason why you shouldn't make it, but you must be willing to accept the odds. At present there are twenty-four major-league baseball teams, twelve each in the National League and the American League. After the first two months or so of the season, each team is limited to keeping twenty-five players on

23

Some Little League players have
made it all the way to the top.

its roster. Thus, there are six hundred active players
in the major leagues—a mere six hundred out of many
thousands of ambitious young men trying to get into
the big leagues. Below the majors, however, there is a
vast network of minor leagues. Most players must
work their way up through various levels of the minors
in order to get a chance at the big time.

Normally you start out playing sandlot or Little
League ball. You move up through school teams and
various summer-league teams. Perhaps during some
high-school or college game you are spotted by a base-

ball scout. If you have done your homework and sharpened your skills, you may be invited to try out in the bush leagues, the bottom of the minor-league ladder. If you are paid at all, it will be very little. You will travel by bus, stay in second-class hotels, eat hamburger, and play your heart out. With hard work, you may skip a rung or two on the minor-league ladder and move into A, AA, or Triple A baseball. These are the top levels of the minor-league clubs. They usually serve as the gateway into the majors. Despite the odds, if you keep in shape and improve your skills, you have as good a chance as the next guy to go all the way to the top.

The best advice, however, is to play only for the present. As time goes on, if you can run, hit, throw, catch, and, importantly, think, the chance to move up will come your way. You won't have to go looking for it.

To get the most fun out of baseball, you should be willing and eager to keep practicing and learning the fine points of the game. Although you may not make first string immediately, maybe next year you will, or the year after that. At the very least you will strengthen yourself physically.

Working with the umpires—not against them—
is an important part of the game.

Part of training is to rid yourself of the tendency to lay blame on someone else. Arguing with an umpire is a mistake. A protest gets you nowhere and is usually a weak alibi for your own shortcomings. Razzing or bench jockeying opposing players also is a cover-up for the weaknesses on your own team. Using the same energies to encourage your own teammates is much better.

Constant skull sessions are an important part of baseball practice. For example, the bases are loaded. There are no outs. It is late in the game. Your team leads by four runs. As shortstop, you stab a hard-hit grounder to your left. What do you do with it? Go for the close force at home, and maybe cut off a run? Peg to first for an easy out? No indeed, you go for two. Second to first. Giving up a run is less important than cleaning off some of the bases and stopping a rally.

A good coach will put you through a lot of such situation drills, or pressure drills. Once studied and learned, they can then be tried out during actual prac-

Now matter how skilled he may be, a player can always benefit from good coaching.

tice. Eventually you instinctively do the right thing in any of the countless game situations where there is no time to hesitate and ponder your moves. Using your head is as important to your game as being able to catch or throw the ball.

You go out for the school baseball team with the idea of pegging out opposing players and scoring runs. However, you will find yourself doing a lot of things

Running is the most important exercise.

that are much less exciting. You will go through many exercises aimed to increase your strength, improve your speed and timing, and sharpen your reflexes.

Of all the exercises, running is the most important. You must run, run, run. It builds your wind. It strengthens your legs. It firms up the muscles all through your body. It's the best all-around exercise you can do. If you live within, say, a mile of school, running the distance will pay off on the baseball diamond. Running when on an errand also will help you be ready when you need extra endurance or added speed during late innings. Whether you pitch, catch, play the infield or outfield, running will be a big part of your career as long as you play baseball.

A typical practice session begins with about a quarter-mile fast jog around the track or several trips around the base paths. To further loosen your muscles, you go through five minutes or so of jumping and stretching calisthenics: knee bends, sit-ups, and torso twists. Jump-rope exercise increases endurance, agility, balance, quickness, and concentration—all of which help your game. Hanging loosely from horizontal bars and twisting your body is great for stretching the muscles. But, to prevent strain, do so only after you have

It is important to stretch and loosen
the muscles before starting a game.

warmed up. Then, before you cool off, pair off with a
teammate and take turns doing a forty-yard wheelbarrow exercise. He holds your legs while you walk on
your arms. This drill gives your arm, shoulder, and
back muscles a workout.

Now it's time to bring out the baseballs. You and the
other players form two lines about fifty feet apart and
play catch. After a few minutes you back away to a

30

hundred feet, later to a hundred and fifty feet. While playing catch you throw with a purpose, instead of simply lobbing the ball. Put a bit of mustard on each throw, and aim for a target, such as your teammate's belt buckle. In this way you will develop the throwing control so important to baseball.

The wheelbarrow is good muscle-building exercise.

Playing "pepper" helps improve
skills with both bat and mitt.

You may follow up this session with several minutes
of playing "pepper," tossing a ball at short range and
having the batter pop it back with a half swing. This
practice helps bat control and quickness with the glove.

After about a half hour of such warm-up drills, you
get the chance to practice individual skills. Maybe you
need to strengthen your hitting. Batting practice is in

Pulling a bat against tension
develops muscles and improves form.

order. If your shoulders, arms, and wrists are not
strong enough to swing the bat properly, try a weighted
bat for a while. When you finish, the normal bat will
seem feather light.

Try using a bat that has a rope tied to it at the top
and is held in tension by a teammate. There are even
automatic pulley tension devices, such as Exer-genies,

which require you to swing a bat against a resisting force. This isometric type of exercise can improve the strength and form of your swing greatly.

Pitchers can make use of isometrics, too. They go through pitching motions with a ball attached to a cord and played out under tension in the same way that the bat was tethered.

There are numerous other methods and devices for

Pitchers benefit from slow motion isometric exercises to strengthen arm and wrist action.

training and practice. Lifting weights is good, if you do so without excess strain. Increasing finger strength is important to both batting and throwing. There are the familiar coil-spring hand exercisers available at sporting-goods stores. But there are simpler ways. The great Ted Williams used to carry small rubber balls around with him, squeezing them absently as he went about his affairs off the playing field.

Weighted balls are used in throwing practice. Weighing slightly over one pound, they are considerably heavier than the normal five ounces. Such balls, thrown at a nearby padded screen, help you develop your throwing or pitching form and motion.

The methods and gimmicks used by players to develop their strengths and skills are virtually endless. Their value, of course, is not measured by the cost or complexity of the device, but by the result. Not having a weighted bat to swing, a horizontal bar from which to hang, or a pitching machine for batting practice is no excuse. All you need is willpower. You always can find a simple way to exercise and improve your game.

After warm-up and individual practice, your team takes to the field for hitting practice, base running, and running through defensive plays that are likely to occur

Sliding practice helps prevent
possible injuries on the diamond.

during actual games. Next to the games themselves, these teamwork exercises under gamelike situations are the most fun. They also reveal just how well you have trained and mastered your skills. You can be sure that the coach is keeping his eyes on your every move during each drill, for he picks his first-string players from what he sees during practice.

The teamwork drills may wind up with sliding practice in a sandpit or some other soft surface. A popular device often used is called a Slip 'n Slide. This rig is simply a silicon-treated sheet of plastic about four feet wide and twenty feet long. When it is wet, it becomes very slippery. After peeling down to your shorts, you make a run at it. You take off, hitting the plastic in correct sliding position with your body twisted on one side. The bottom leg is bent under you, and the top leg hooks or reaches straight out for an imaginary bag. Or else you come in headfirst. You get wet. But you escape skin burns or strawberries and avoid the grind of dirt and gravel into your hide.

And that ends the day's practice. It is time to head for the showers. But don't walk . . . run!

third inning
PITCHING

The most crucial part of any baseball game is the never-ending contest between pitcher and batter. It is a duel between a good pitching arm and a well-swung bat, but it is even more a battle of wits.

There really is no mold into which pitchers fit. The tall fellows with long, loose muscles seem able to get more speed and put more stuff on the ball, but this observation does not rule out the short pitcher. Anyone who has extra determination and the ability to hit the corners, mix up his pitches, and generally baffle the batters can be a good pitcher. Still, these days, when power pitching is considered to be about seventy-five percent of a team's defense, the strong, rangy man with the long arm and whiplike speed usually gets the mound assignment.

To become a successful pitcher you must learn three types of control: self-control, body control, and ball control. If you complain a lot, if you let your temper fly, if you look for alibis, your playing is sure to suffer. Unless you can restrain your emotions and keep cool under pressure, you probably won't get a chance on the mound. You may have noticed that a coach usually will jerk a pitcher who grouses, throws the resin bag, bellows at the umpire, or angrily kicks dirt. The coach knows that such a loss of self-control has ruined that pitcher's game for the day. So keep calm.

Body control means being able to coordinate your muscles and mind so they work like a well-oiled machine. Many players are naturally coordinated, but everyone can improve his body control with practice.

If you decide that pitcher is the position you want to play, proceed slowly. Don't go right out and start trying to throw curves. Without proper training you can hurt your arm and elbow and cut short what might have been a promising career in baseball. Lay off the curve, at least until you are well into your teens. Even then be sure you are properly coached before trying it.

Build up your arm with regular exercise. Try never to overdo the drill, yet don't be too willing to quit at the first signs of fatigue. When you throw, go through the full motion of pitching, and always throw at a target. Pitch to a plate of some sort. Getting a batter to stand in position is also helpful.

Of course, keep running. Running is as important to a pitcher as to anyone else on the team. Running strengthens your overall stamina. Unless the rest of your body and limbs are strong, your pitching arm won't do you a bit of good. Any sensible exercise such as bicycling, swimming, going up stairs two at a time, doing calisthenics, working out with weights or on the bars will add to your strength and body control. The most important part of pitching is being able to put the ball where you want it. You can have the speed of white lightning or be able to bend a curve around a barrel, but unless you can hit a target at the far end of the throw, you have nothing that a ball team can use.

So you start out easily. You pick your target, such as the catcher's left knee or the letters on his uniform. His mitt, of course, is the most commonly used mark.

40

Or you may "throw at the strings." When this method is followed, the average strike zone is outlined with twine. It is seventeen inches wide, the official width of home plate. It is about a yard high, from average knee height to average armpit level.

First you start out developing up-and-down control. Don't worry about inside and outside pitches, or clip-

A strike zone outlined with string makes
a fine practice target for a pitcher.

ping the corners. Just try to get the ball squarely over the plate, keeping it low within the strike zone. The low pitches are the "money pitches" in baseball. They are the hardest to see, hardest to reach, hardest to hit, and even when hit usually result in a ground ball to an infielder.

So develop the habit of keeping your pitches low. As your control improves you can start putting more speed on the ball. Once your pitching comes alive, you will need very little extra effort to hit the edges or the corners of the plate. When pitches are working well, they almost have eyes of their own.

You will be wise to limit yourself to three basic pitches, which is what most major leaguers rely on. They are the fast ball, the curve ball, and the change-up. Leave the trick, or "junk," pitches—sliders, screwballs, fork balls, and knucklers—for a later time. With the exception of the knuckler, most of them are only slight variations of the three basic pitches anyway. The bread-and-butter pitch is the fast ball. You use it to challenge the batter who digs in at the plate, determined to knock the cover off the ball.

You take your catcher's sign—one finger for the fast ball. You go into your windup. You hide the ball in

42

Left: The knuckle ball
Right: The basic fastball grip

your glove while you grip it on the seams with your
index and middle fingers. Some fast-ball pitchers grip
along the seams, others across the seams. The only rule
is to use the grip that works best for you. Your thumb
also rests firmly on the seams under the ball. Your

fourth and little fingers fold in naturally toward the palm of your hand.

Your pivot foot, on the same side as your pitching arm, toes the rubber that is the pitcher's plate. You go into your windup, leaning back and twisting your body,

The windup builds momentum and aids body control.

giving the batter a view of your hip pocket. Then you start to uncoil, bringing the ball out of your glove and shifting all of your momentum forward. You thrust your pivot foot hard against the inside of the rubber and bend your knee. You heave your striding leg high,

Get the striding leg up,
and thrust off with the pivot foot.

as though you were going to stick your foot in the batter's face.

At the same time you swing your arm forward in a
three-quarter overhand arc. Your body, shoulder, arm,
and wrist work in unison with the single purpose of

Letting everything out toward home plate

releasing the ball at maximum speed. You let it go, whipping the wrist and flinging the ball straight off your fingertips. Its natural backspin will cause the ball to rise slightly as it nears the plate.

As the ball leaves your fingers, you continue your

Once started for the plate,
concentrate completely on the pitch.

follow-through motion. Your pitching hand finishes its long sweep, and you are virtually "picking grass." You land gently on the toes of your striding foot, bending your knee to help absorb the shock.

During this time you keep your head level and your

A good follow-through gets the body
low to the ground and in balance.

eyes on your target. As you end the follow-through, you bring your pivot foot forward off the rubber so you are facing the batter and ready to field anything hit your way. You also are ready to break toward first base in case anything is hit to your left.

But the pitch is a good one, and the batter swings and misses. He backs up a little deeper in the batter's box and scratches out new toeholds with his cleats. The new position is intended to give him an extra fraction of a second to get a better look at your fast ball.

So you cross him up and feed him a curve. (Remember, no curves until your teens.) As always, you hide the ball in your glove, showing no white until the pitch is under way. You grip the seams, use the same windup, and follow the same motion you would as with any other pitch. Only you release the ball with a sharp out-and-down snap of the wrist, spinning it off the top of your index finger.

The curve ball travels at much less speed than the fast ball. It veers down and away from the batter. Again his bat whiffs empty air.

With a count of no balls and two strikes, you can afford to tempt him. But he doesn't bite, and you waste an inside fast ball and a low curve.

The curve uses extreme amounts
of wrist and elbow action.

You need to get the next one in, and since the batter probably figures your fast ball is your best pitch, he gets set for it. So, in the battle of wits, you shake off your catcher's sign for a fast ball and nod slightly as he shows you three fingers, calling for your third basic pitch, the change-up.

Now you toe the pitching rubber for the two-two pitch. You take your natural windup and lean back. Then you uncoil as you hurl the ball toward the plate.

50

But the big difference is that you have held the ball a bit deeper in your hand, and you open your fingers a little early in order to release the ball just short of the final whip and wrist action given your other two pitches. And thus the change-up, neither a fast ball nor a curve, but a little of both, heads toward the plate at reduced speed.

The difference is just enough to spoil the batter's timing. However, he does get a small piece of it with the tip of his bat. The grounder spins slowly down the first-base line, and neither you nor the catcher are able to field it in time to throw out the batter.

At this point, with a man on base, you must forget your windup and pitch from a stretch. You stand on the mound with your pivot foot firmly set against the forward edge of the rubber, hiding the gripped ball in the pocket of your glove. You stretch both arms over your head, bring them down slowly to chest level, and pause there for the second that is required by the rules in order not to be guilty of a balk.

The runner dances off first base, threatening to steal second and also trying to make you jittery and uncertain. You look over your shoulder and stare him back to the base. (If you are left-handed, of course,

51

you are facing him and he will be more careful of his lead.) If he doesn't go back or if he takes too big a lead, step toward the base and try to pick him off with a quick, low throw to the first sacker. But once you

From his stretch position, the pitcher keeps
a close, threatening watch on the runner at first.

make up your mind to attempt the pick-off at first, you must continue the motion and make the throw. Otherwise, you will be called for a balk, and the runner will get a free trip to second.

On the other hand, suppose that you have been able to stare the runner back close to the base. You decide to finish your pitch. Now forget the runner completely. Put all of your mind and body into the pitch. To split your attention between pitch and runner would ruin your concentration and no doubt spoil your throw. You heave back, then fling the ball toward the catcher's waiting glove, using the same pitching principles as before: eyes on the target, bent knee, and smooth follow-through.

And so your duel with the batters continues. You try never to let the batter outguess you. You mix up your pitches. You pitch to different targets. You change your speed and rhythm to spoil the batter's timing. You try to keep him off-balance. You don't let up on the weak hitters. Too often they are the ones who get the clutch hits that score the base runners.

Above all, don't worry about the good hitters. Any hitter can sense a pitcher's fear, and he will dig in his toes and knock you off the mound. You must be confident that you can strike out any batter who faces you. Confidence will give each pitch the extra zing it needs.

The position of pitcher is a challenging one to play on any team. Pitching requires a great deal of skill and practice, but it is worth trying if you are willing to meet its demands.

fourth inning
CATCHING

If you have a lot of energy and are a real workhorse, catching behind the plate may be the best position for you. Don't believe that old wheeze about the big mitt, the shin guards, the chest protector, and the mask being "the tools of ignorance." To be a catcher you must have one of the nimblest minds on the diamond. You also have to be able to take charge and control the game.

You seldom rest. You back up plays, chatter encouragement to your pitcher, or shout instructions to the fielders. And that says nothing of the sheer skill you must have for catching and throwing the baseball.

Of course, you cannot be bat shy, for it swings quite near as you crouch close in behind the plate. Actually, although the position looks dangerous to the bystander, catchers seldom get nicked by a bat. As a hitter strides into his swing, the arc of the bat pulls well away from the catcher's hands or head. In fact, with your equip-

The catcher is the anchor man of a ball team.

ment for protection, you take much less of a battering than many think.

As the pitch comes at you, you simply pay no attention to the bat. You concentrate fully on keeping the ball from getting past you. If you can't quite get your mitt on it, your duty is to lunge out for the ball, block it with your body, or do whatever is necessary to knock it down and keep it in play out in front of you.

A person of almost any size can become a catcher. You need quick reflexes, a strong arm, strong legs, and good, flexible knees, which you will bend much of the time as you crouch to catch and straighten up to throw. Also, you should be right-handed.

During the game, you squat behind the plate. You study the batter and give the sign to the pitcher. You keep the sign simple, holding your right fist in near your crotch, well hidden from view by any member of the opposing team. You thrust one finger down for a fast ball, two for a curve, or three for a change-up, maybe waggle four fingers for a pitchout. Then, getting ready to receive the pitch, you rise slightly, and reach forward with your mitt to give the pitcher a target.

You keep your bare, or "meat," hand at the edge of your mitt, fingers folded loosely out of the way to

Catcher's signs are kept simple
and hidden from general view.

prevent injury. If, as many catchers do these days, you use a "hinged" mitt that has a break in the outer rim, you may simply catch the ball one-handed. However, in most cases using the right hand to clamp over the ball and keep it from bouncing out is a good idea.

Also, whether or not there is a runner on base, you should get into the habit of grabbing the ball out of the mitt and stepping forward with your left foot, ready to throw.

When you throw, you must do so quickly. There is no time to wind up. If you aim at second, your throw has to cover some 127 feet while the runner, who takes off with the pitch, is about ready to go into his slide. So you must cock your arm quickly, stride forward, and throw from behind your ear. You must throw as

Using the small, "hinged" glove, many catchers keep their "meat hand" out of harm's way.

hard as you can, and with confidence. Throw to just above the bag or a little to the runner's side, and keep the throw low.

Any bunted ball you can handle, you chase down and round up with both hands, stopping it with your mitt, then scooping it up with your throwing hand. You concentrate on the ball, not the runner. Unless you get solid control of the ball, there is nothing you can do about the runner anyway. If the bunt is along the first-base line, you must leap to one side or the other of the running path in order to snap a throw to first without hitting the runner with the ball.

As a catcher, you must be able to judge and handle towering foul balls. With wind and sun and nearby bleachers, this play is not easy to execute. A pop foul usually has a lot of spin on it and, caught in swirling air currents, can do some crazy things. Often you can tell by the sound of the bat if the foul is a simple tip headed straight for the backstop or whether it is popped up. Your first job on a pop-up is to locate the ball. You tear your mask off to get a better view. But you don't get rid of your mask until you see the ball. Then, so you won't trip over it, you toss the mask in a direction away from the path you will take in chasing the foul.

60

A few catchers prefer making
basket-type catches of foul balls.

You get under the ball as quickly as you can. In fact,
you try to get slightly behind it, so you can catch it
moving forward. You must adjust your position so the
wind cannot carry the ball out of your reach. Nor do
you want to lose it in the sun. You may tip the mitt up

A catcher cannot be afraid of . . .

so the ball pops into the basketlike pocket. Or you may catch with the mitt up at eye level. In either case, you clamp your right hand over it as quickly as possible, for spinning balls too often pop right back out of mitts.

One of your other big jobs is to guard home plate

against a runner bent on scoring. This task is often a matter of force meeting force. The whole purpose of the runner is to touch that plate, come high water or plague of locusts. If he has to he will knock you down to do so.

But you needn't give him the chance. As the ball comes toward you from some infielder or outfielder, you stand in front of the plate, guarding the base line but not blocking it. You are not allowed to block the base line unless you have the ball, or you can be called for interference. So you let part of the plate show as bait to the runner. Once you get the ball, you apply the tag firmly. Clutch the ball tightly in your right hand but protect it in the pocket of your mitt. Tag with the back

. . . a little body contact now and then.

Making the tag at home

of the mitt so the ball will not be jarred out of your grip.

The catcher's job is varied and exciting. If it is true, as some say, that seventy-five percent of a team's defense depends on good pitching, perhaps half of the credit should go to good catching. Unless the pitcher and the catcher work together as a solid battery, there can be no victory.

In fact, one of your most important jobs is to help the pitcher. You must keep building him up and boosting his morale, particularly when his confidence begins to get shaky after giving up several hits, or when he is trying to recover his control after a costly wild pitch. Even when he is down, your job is to make him believe that he still has his stuff and that his next pitch will be

Pitcher and catcher work together.

the greatest in the world. You need to know his best pitches. If his fast ball is working that day, give him plenty of chances to throw it. If his curve isn't bending, lay off it and call for the change-up.

Not only must you know your own pitcher, you must remember the strengths and weaknesses of the opposing batters. Perhaps you haven't had a real chance to study them; you have no "book" on them. Still, there are little things that will tip you off to what the batter intends to do on the next pitch.

If he stands back from the plate and opens his stance by dropping his forward foot back in the box, he is either worried about getting hit by a close pitch or is planning to pull the ball, that is, hit it toward left field if he is a right-handed batter, toward right field if he is left-handed. Call for an outside pitch, and he probably won't be able to reach it. If he crowds the plate, a free swinger anxious to clobber anything that comes near the strike zone, call for a fast inside pitch to brush him back and make him think twice. If there are runners on base and a bunt seems likely, you can call for a pitchout, a ball that is deliberately wide of the plate so the batter cannot hit it. Or you can ask for a high, inside fast ball that he will most likely pop up for an easy out.

These are but a few of the situations that you work out with your battery mate, the pitcher. As the field general on most occasions, you keep your teammates reminded of the number of outs. You direct traffic on the infield around home plate. When you know the batters' habits, you set the outfielders where you think the ball will be hit. Having the best view of what's taking place on the diamond, you yell to the pitcher or infielder handling a bunt where to throw the ball to get the force on the front runners or the tag on the single runner. You call who should handle pop flies.

You often back up plays on first base. But, with runners on base, you never leave home plate unguarded. You are, in fact, in on almost every play. No one can ever accuse a catcher of choosing an easy job. However, the fun and importance of playing the position are well worth the effort.

67

fifth inning
HITTING

Your job when you step into the batter's box is to keep
any pitch from passing untouched through the strike
zone, which you are guarding. Your main weapon is
your bat, a chunk of rounded hardwood about a yard
long. Choosing it carefully is important. Too many
young players make the mistake of picking a massive
club with the idea of smacking towering fly balls over
distant fences. Later they find that they aren't strong
enough to whip it around in time to meet the ball.
Insead of hitting triples or home runs, they end up
striking out or swinging late.

68

Although a bat can be up to forty-two inches long, you probably will find thirty-two to thirty-five inches of seasoned ash sufficient. Many major leaguers use shorter lengths. Since a bat weighs about an ounce per inch, the total weight amounts to a couple of pounds or so. A bat with a thin handle helps wrist action. Push batters and spot hitters usually can control a large-handled bat more easily.

Duplicating lathes make exact copies
of whatever bat suits a player best.

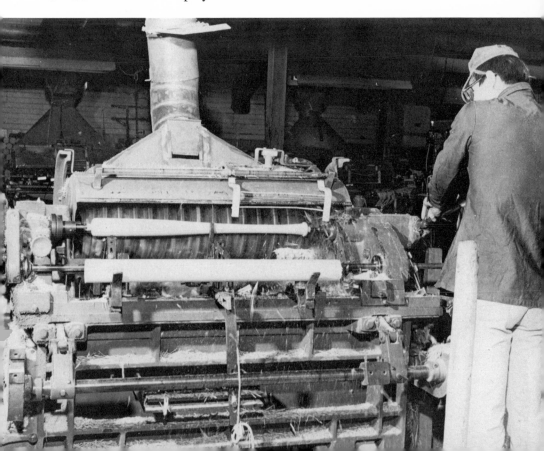

So try out bats of several different lengths and weights. You will discover which is most comfortable and suits you best. Use it. Use it as long as it does the job for you. The job, of course, is to "hit 'em where they ain't." And that doesn't mean hitting pitches into the left-field bleachers. It means bunting them, or hitting them past the infielders, through the holes, just over their heads, anyplace where "they ain't." For every

Pitching machines help players improve their hitting.

player who can pole out an occasional home run, there are a dozen steady hitters who can pop a needed line drive past the second baseman or lay down an important bunt.

When you have picked your bat, you are ready to start swinging it. By now you no doubt have strengthened yourself through steady training. To swing a bat properly and with enough power to get results, you

Players usually sharpen up their hitting with plenty of batting cage practice.

need strength—hands, wrists, arms, shoulders, and back.

You step into the batter's box and take your stance. To determine just how near to the plate you should stand, take a slow practice swing and see if the tip of your bat reaches the far edge of the plate. In this manner you can be sure that the bat will cover the entire strike zone and the fat of the bat—where the best hits come from—swings through the middle of the strike area.

You should hold the bat firmly, but don't squeeze it. Don't grip it in the palm of your hands, but with your fingers which will guide its swing. If you are a power hitter, hold the bat at the end with the heel of your lower hand against the knob. If you are a placement hitter, or if the balance seems more comfortable, choke up a few inches on the handle. You may lose about five percent of power, but you will gain about twenty-five percent in bat control. Don't let anyone tell you that choking up on a bat is for amateurs. Plenty of the big-league pros do, and with great success.

A firm stance in the batter's box is important. Here, again, test several stances and decide which is most comfortable. Keep your feet fairly parallel to the side

This batter uses an extreme closed stance, thrusting
his front foot much closer to the plate than the other.

lines of the batter's box. Spread them fourteen to eigh-
teen inches apart. Plant your feet firmly, even if you
have to dig in with your cleats to do so. Work on this
stance. It will have much to do with your stride into the
ball and the rhythm and timing of your swing.

When you have taken your stance, stand with your
weight on your rear foot. Keep your elbows out away

73

from your body, and hold the bat up off your rear shoulder. Don't stand waggling the bat as if threatening to knock the leather off the first pitch that comes your way. If you do, you stand a good chance of getting caught off-balance by a heady pitcher. Hold the bat steady and in such a way that the trademark will be up as the bat passes through the strike zone. Thus, you will take advantage of the strong grain of the wood and avoid breaking bats.

When you are in your stance, your shoulders and hips should be straight, and your knees slightly flexed. You may bend a little forward, but don't crouch or lean out over the plate. Keep the bat reasonably high, but not awkwardly so. Swinging down for a low pitch is easier than swinging up for a high one.

So you are all set and waiting as the pitcher goes into his windup. Lock your eyes on the ball while it is in the pitcher's hand, even though a good pitcher will hide it in his glove as long as he possibly can.

Repeat: Keep your eye on the ball!

Now you see it leave the pitcher's fingers and speed toward you. You have about one half of a second to determine what kind of a pitch it is. You also must decide whether or not it will come into the strike zone and just what you are going to do about it if it does. Even while you are making up your mind you must start moving. You start your straight, short stride in the direction of the ball. Pushing off with your rear foot, you shift your momentum forward. But as yet you haven't made up your mind whether or not the pitch is a strike. So you hold back on your swing as long as you can.

Then, when it is less than a dozen feet from the plate,

The smooth, rhythmic power hitting
that produces consistently good results

you see that the ball is coming into the strike zone. You start your swing with your arms and shoulders. You pivot your hips to carry through with the added motion of your body. Keep your front shoulder up so your bat will stay level. Hold your head steady, and don't, *don't* take your eyes off the ball! Follow it, seam by seam, all the way.

About the time the ball is a foot or so in front of the plate and the bat comes around to meet it, you shift

During the entire swing and follow-through, eyes must stay on the ball.

your weight onto your front foot, planting it firmly on the ground. Bat meets ball just in front of the plate. You uncock your wrists at the moment of contact, whipping the bat right on through the ball. Your front leg is stiff, and you don't bend it until well into the follow-through.

By that time the ball is on its outward way. But you are not paying attention to it. Your interest shifts from hitting the ball to getting on base.

The instant the ball is hit,
the batter must take off for first base.

One of the main things to remember about batting is that there are few hard-and-fast rules that you must follow. Still, a basic one is to keep your eye on the ball. And there are several others, like staying on your toes and never on your heels. "There are no heels in baseball," is a popular saying. Keep your swing as level as possible, and put your whole self into it. Pull the bat through with your left hand (for right-handed hitters) and guide it as you push through with your right hand. Your arms should be fully extended as you swing the bat across the plate. Don't chop down or try to uppercut the ball. If that's the only way you can reach a pitch, it's probably out of the strike zone anyway.

A word of caution: Don't swing as hard as you can. Swing smoothly and hold your form. The results will be better and more consistent than the occasional balls hit into orbit by an all-or-nothing free swinger.

Bunting is an important part of batting. To lay down a bunt, you decide first in which direction you want it to go. Usually you try to dump it down one of the base lines, giving an infielder as hard a chase and as long a throw as possible.

On many bunts there is no real reason to hide what

Bunting must be learned as an important part of baseball.

you intend to do. With runners on first and second and no outs and the score tied, everybody in the ball park knows that you will be laying down a sacrifice bunt to move the runners out of double-play danger. So you can commit yourself early, even during the pitcher's windup, if you feel the extra time to get ready will be helpful.

Normally, though, you wait until he starts his pitch. As the ball approaches, you bring your back foot up even with your front foot. You square away, facing the pitcher. You hold the bat loose and level. Then you slide your top hand out to the label of the bat, cradling it loosely in a *V* made by your thumb and index finger.

You don't swing the bat or even push it at the ball. You let the ball come to the bat. If the pitch is a fast ball coming within the strike zone, you let the bat give a little as the ball hits it. In this way you deaden the impact and keep the bunt from rolling too far and fast, making it easy to field. Ideally your bunt should travel about a third of the way down the base line and die. Then someone has to chase it. He will be lucky if he can scoop it up in time to throw you out. The other base runners for whom you are making the sacrifice almost certainly will move ahead safely.

With runners on first and second, your best bunt is down the third-base line, forcing the third baseman to come in and field it. He not only leaves his base un-guarded but has the long throw to first. When drag bunting for a base hit, don't commit yourself until the last possible moment. Probably you will catch the de-fense unprepared. You slide your top hand only a little way up the bat handle and either push or drag the ball toward one of the holes in the infield. The gaps toward second and shortstop are particularly vulnerable when those infielders are playing deep. Still, you must soften the contact of bat on ball, so the bunt doesn't have too much zip and reach them too soon.

Instead of turning their feet toward the pitcher, most big-leaguers now simply pivot their feet and square their shoulders and hips. Thus they aren't giving themselves away any sooner than necessary. Bunting is done in a more continuous motion, with the bat coming to full pause just before the ball reaches it.

The mental attitude you take to the plate with you is as important as the mechanics of batting. You should try to outthink, not outguess, the pitcher. Know the pitcher's weaknesses and strengths. Try to get ahead in the count so he will have to feed you his fat strike. And be ready for it. In fact, be ready for anything. Remember, you are at the plate to hit, not to get a base on balls. Guard that plate at all times.

Be confident. Challenge the pitcher. Make him pitch the ball you want. Show him that you can hit the best strike he ever threw.

Keep swinging that bat!

sixth inning
RUNNING THE BASES

Runs are scored, naturally, with your legs. No matter how good you are with the bat, unless you can outrun throws, steal a base now and then, and slide in under tags, your ability to hit the ball may have little value.

Since the shortest distance between two points is a straight line, that is how you should run the ninety-foot sprints between bases—except for slight variations now and then. For instance, as soon as you hit the ball, you dig for first base. You churn as fast as you can, straight down the three-foot wide base path, trying for a single.

But you must not think *single*. Always think *double*!

82

Don't pull up on first, satisfied. Unless it is one of those close plays when you run straight down the base line and "through" the base, swing a little to your right as you approach the bag. Then veer back to your left, rounding off the corner. Touch the inside corner of the base with your left foot, and push off for second. Don't, however, be too particular about using your left foot. Keep from breaking stride and use whichever foot is there first. By thinking in terms of a double, you are

Hit the nearest corner of first
base and push off for second.

Always run your hardest.

ready to take advantage of any bobble of the ball or any loafing on the part of the defense. If you are going to be held to a single, make the opponents turn you back. Don't give up voluntarily.

Whenever you reach a base, be ready to go on. But don't do so carelessly, because once you have rounded a base you are subject to a tag. Even on first base, which you are allowed to overrun straight ahead, if you make your turn and indicate that you may try for second, you are fair game for a tag.

Take a lead, and be balanced and ready to go.

Always run your hardest, even on sure grounders to the infield or easy pop flies. There is always the chance for an error or bad defensive judgment. Championships have been lost by runners who gave up too soon.

Once you are on first base, you begin thinking about getting to second, continuing your battle of wits with the pitcher. Take your lead only after the pitcher has his foot on the rubber and is ready to go into his stretch. How far you edge off the base depends on how good an arm he has and how well he makes the pick-

Beware of the pick-off.

off play. If he is a left-hander you have to be more careful, since he is facing you and can peg quickly to first.

Ease yourself off the base—maybe six or seven feet —but be careful not to get so far that you can get caught by a good pick-off throw. Move smoothly away from the bag. Don't dance around. A good pitcher will trap you in the middle of a pirouette or when you're leaning toward second base. Stay just within range, so you can return to the bag ahead of any throw.

Stealing bases is a big part of the game. A stolen base

Headfirst into a successful steal

often makes the difference between defeat and victory. Whether the sign comes from your coach or you go it on your own, the big secret is to get a jump on the pitch. Study the pitcher's moves. Watch his striding foot. He must move it either toward home plate or toward first base. As soon as he comes out of his stretch and commits himself to a pitching motion toward the plate, take off for all you are worth. He can't change his mind midway; it would be a balk, and you would be awarded the next base automatically.

87

Chances are that any catcher worth his shin guards will be able to gun the ball to second before you arrive. But you have to be tagged by the baseman. To avoid him, you need to slide under or away from the tag.

As you approach the base, you note to which side of the bag the baseman has shifted in order to catch the throw. Glide, don't leap or jump into your slide. Stay low. Crook your bottom leg and slide in on your

The runner starts his slide
as the ball approaches the baseman.

padded thigh. Reach out for the bag with the foot of your straight top leg. Hold your hands up and out of harm's way. Once your foot makes contact, bend your knee and hook your body away from the baseman's tag. Just be sure you keep contact with the base at all times.

The bent leg slide is a variation of the hook slide. You don't lie as far back on the ground, but approach

A good hook slide into home plate

the base semierect and ever alert. As soon as your out-stretched foot touches the bag, you use it as leverage to pop back up onto your feet, ready to head for the next base at the slightest opportunity.

On some occasions, such as getting back to a base to beat a pick-off play, the headfirst slide is most successful. You need only get a finger on any part of the bag, especially the near back corner, to avoid the tag. But high-speed headfirst sliding is riskier than the feet-first slides. Nevertheless, a determined player will get a base any way he can.

Once you make up your mind and start your slide, don't change. Hit the dirt and follow through. Hesitation can throw your timing off and cause a twisted ankle or some other injury.

As a base runner you should be willing to take some chances in order to advance toward home, but not foolish ones. Generally you can move up a base or two on hits that go behind you. If, however, you are on second base, and the ball goes to the shortstop, your chances for advancing to third are slim. The infielder can bluff you back and still make his throw to first in time to catch the runner.

Baseball running requires a lot of good judgment,

Getting home the hard way

for in spite of the help from a base coach, you are the only one who really can decide whether the risk is worth the possible gain. To attempt stealing third when there are two outs, for example, is foolish. A hit will score you anyway, so why take a chance of ending the inning?

On long fly balls to the outfield, you must judge whether to tag up, that is, touch the base after the ball is caught, and try to advance. Or you may decide to go halfway to the next base in the hope that the catch will not be made and that you can pick up two bases on the play. Just don't get too far away from the bag, or

Stalling a rundown

an outfielder with a good arm may pick you off before you can get back.

Speaking of tagging up, don't forget that you can advance on a caught foul fly as well as on any fly ball. So tag up on long foul balls or those that the catcher has to race to the backstop to get. Once you have sized up the situation—and fielders sometimes are caught napping in this one—you may be able to take an extra base after the catch.

Once in a while you may get caught between bases in a rundown. By no means give up and allow yourself to be tagged without a struggle. Keep the rundown going as long as you can. It may give the other runner or runners the chance to take an extra base. Remember that the runner in front "owns" the base. Keep your eye on him. Don't overrun him, or you will be tagged easily for an out.

Baserunning is a big part of the fun in baseball. It gives you a chance to think for yourself and move fast. Put your best effort into it and be a real winner.

seventh inning
PLAYING THE INFIELD

To play the infield you need sure hands, a strong arm, fast reflexes, lots of drive, and a good head. Today the new synthetic turfs make the balls more lively, which further increases the need for an infielder to be quick and to time his moves skillfully.

Each position of the infield—first base, second base, third base, and shortstop—has its special needs. But by and large the infield plays as a unit: four guys determined to prevent hits and keep runners off the bases.

If you are a left-hander, first base is by far your best position. Being a lefty means your glove hand will be

on the diamond side for tag plays. Also, since most of
your throws will be to your right, you are already in
position to peg the ball without having to twist or pivot.
There are good right-handed first basemen in any

Often the first baseman needs to stretch way up . . .

. . . and far out.

league, of course, but southpaws have an advantage.

As first baseman you have to be able to receive throws that are shotgunned all around you. You must be able to stretch far out, leap high, and dig wild throws out of the dirt. You should be able to stand pressure, too, because a first baseman takes an active part in about one third of all defensive plays.

To occupy one of the other three infield positions, you should be right-handed, because most of your plays and throws will be to your left. This direction is the natural one for a right-hander.

96

As second baseman you must be able to move to your left in order to knock down ground balls heading through the slot toward right field. But you must be equally adept at darting to your right to flag down balls that get past the pitcher. You also must be able to drift into short right or center field to take in pop flies that are too shallow for the outfielders to reach. However, if an outfielder calls for the ball, peel off. He can catch it as he comes in more easily than you can

A second baseman poised for action

as you run backward. And, most important, if there are runners on the base paths, the outfielder is in far better position to make a throw.

If you are a holler guy, a real go-getter, think about playing shortstop. Remember, however, that you must cover a big slice of the infield. The shortstop's territory extends all the way from second base to the "hole," that dangerous no-man's-land between shortstop and third base.

A shortstop is always on the move.

You must have a strong arm. Playing back on or near the grass, as you often will, you have the longest throw to first base. Most of the time, in the close contest between your arm and the runner's feet, you have to hurl the ball from whatever position you are in when you catch it. You must be able to throw on the run, often underhand or sidearm. You are lucky if you have time to straighten up and peg an accurate overhand from behind your ear.

One of your big jobs is to team up with the second baseman to make the "keystone combination" for double plays. Being located in the middle, second base is called the keystone of the diamond.

On double plays, depending upon where the ball is hit, you trade off as pivot man, taking the throw for a force-out at second, jumping clear of the slide, and snapping the ball on to first in time to complete the play. This is one of the most challenging and exciting plays in baseball, and, whenever there is a man on first base and fewer than two outs, everyone in the infield should think double-double-double. Get two!

As shortstop you are in the best position to direct traffic in the infield the way the catcher does around the home-plate area. Call for the ball loud and clear if you

99

The "keystone combination" at work

think you can handle it. But shout to the other basemen to "Take it! Take it!" if one of them has a little
better chance at it—or if he can catch it looking away
from a blinding sun.

Third base also has its special needs. Called the "hot
corner," more ground balls streak down that ninety-
foot base line—and faster and harder—than to any
other part of the diamond. And since you usually play
in close to the bag, a hard-hit ball is on you instantly.

You must think fast and have a quick glove. Obviously you also must have a good arm for the long throw to first base.

Although there are differences in the demands made by each infield position, there are many moves common to all four. Fielding ground balls is one of them.

There is a standard saying, "Play the ball; don't let the ball play you." In other words, don't wait for the

Leaping away from flashing spikes,
a shortstop pegs to first for the double play.

The "hot corner" man must think fast and have a good arm.

ball to come to you. Charge it. You can often time your stride to catch the ball on the big hop, when it is easy to handle. Or you can charge in, nab it on the short hop, and in one fluid motion peg to first. To back up, or to be uncertain and try to snare the ball in midhop, often results in an error. The midhoppers usually are the trickiest to judge and handle.

When at all possible, move into the path of the ball. Keep your glove down, right in the dirt if necessary. There is no excuse for letting a ground ball go through under your glove. As long as your glove is down, even if the ball takes a bad hop, you usually are able to block it with your wrist, arm, or body. Try to get in front of it.

Most important, on all ground balls, bend your knees and stay low, keeping your head and body down. Watch the ball every inch of the way. Don't worry about the runners. There is nothing you can do about them until you get control of the ball. Head down! Eyes on the ball! Look it right into your glove.

Once the ball is in your glove, and if you have caught it with both hands, the simple task of digging it out and pegging to the base is halfway accomplished. By moving forward into the catch, your momentum already is toward first, and you also have cut down on the distance. Get your grip across the seams of the ball and make your throw. But be sure there is someone at the base to catch it. You'd be surprised at how often an infielder who has properly made up his mind beforehand will flip the ball, without looking, to a bag that has been left unattended for some reason.

Don't make a throw if you can see that the runner is going to beat it out. You may be tempted to complete your play and look good. But if you obviously can't get the runner, hold onto the ball and save a possible error. Or bluff a throw and maybe catch some other runner who has been lured off his base.

As an infielder you cannot afford to stand around with hands on your knees, unless it is during a time-out

Stay down with the ball.

period. Your best stance as an infielder is to stand with feet comfortably spread, leaning a little forward on your toes, ready to react in any direction. Flex your knees and let your arms and hands hang loose with both palms opened toward home plate. Expect every ball to come your way, and be ready. Figure out what you will do with the ball when you get it. Plan ahead. A moment's uncertainty often costs a sure out.

After the catch, swing forward into the throw.

If the ball doesn't come to you, find something to do. Back up a base. Get into position to relay or cut off a throw from the outfield. Watch to see that a runner touches each and every base.

Be in on every play! Don't ever loaf.

All infielders must be able to make the tag play. There are two main types of tags. One is the sweeping tag. You use it when you are on the move or the ball is

The tag

off its target. You get hold of the ball any way you can and sweep it down onto the slider's foot or hand before it touches the bag. You usually do so with a quick and deft movement, as you keep your eye on the man to be certain of getting the tag. Keep the ball solidly in your glove. Turn your wrist and make the tag with the back of your glove, not with the ball itself. This technique protects your hand from flashing spikes and keeps the ball from being jarred loose.

The other common way to make a tag, most often used at second and third, is to plant yourself astride the bag while awaiting the throw. By straddling the bag you can move in either direction to reach an off-target throw, and you also are not illegally blocking the base path before you have possession of the ball.

You hold your position and let the throw come to you. Staying as close to the bag as possible, you grab the ball in your glove and hold it firmly with your bare hand. By this time the runner probably is into his slide. Hold the ball down at the edge of the base and let him slide into it. Again, for protection, turn the back of your glove toward him. Only in most unusual situations, where there is no alternative, should you try to tag a runner with the ball exposed in your bare hand.

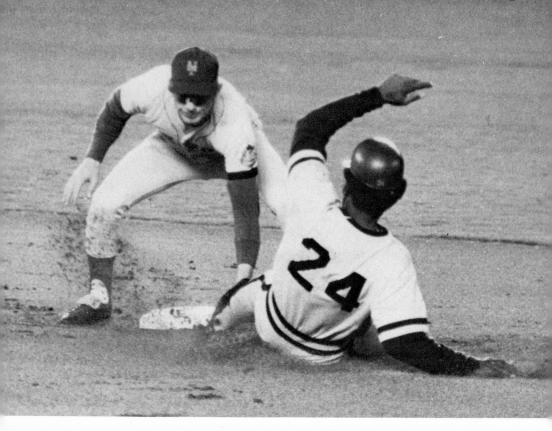

Straddle the bag and let the runner slide into the tag.

Another of your duties as an infielder is to go out on the grass and get into position to relay throws from outfielders. How far you move depends on how far the hit ball went and how good an arm the outfielder has. Try to stay as close to the infield as possible. The relay, or cutoff, man should be able to send a quick, accurate throw anywhere there's a chance to catch a runner.

For a relay, or cutoff, set yourself in line with home plate or whichever base the outfielder is pegging toward. Hold your mitt above your head to give the outfielder a target. Try to know what is going on around you. What are the runners doing? What are your teammates doing? If you're not sure what is happening behind you, listen for the catcher's call. He has a full view of the action.

With a man tagging up on third and perhaps other runners on bases, set your cutoff position between the outfielder and home plate. Give the outfielder his target. You intend to let a good throw go on through to the catcher on one bounce. If the catcher sees that the throw is not going to get the man at home, or at one of the other bases, he will quickly shout, "Cut! Cut!" You intercept the throw and look around for other possibilities. Or the catcher may shout, "Cut! One!" or "Cut! Two! Two!" The call tells you to intercept the ball and peg it immediately to first base or to second.

There is no end to the variety of plays infielders are called on to make. Some are individual plays, but most are team plays. So infielders need to know each player's moves, his strong points and weaknesses. Can he go to his right? Can he handle low throws? The entire infield must be able to work as a unit on double plays and always back each other up.

A good example of this teamwork takes place during a rundown, when an opposing player is caught on a base path. If they back each other up, infielders should be able to trap the runner and tag him out by making one or two throws.

To make a good infielder you have to be aggressive and give the game everything you've got. Chances are you will be glad you did, for the infield is where most of the fast action takes place.

eighth inning
PLAYING THE OUTFIELD

The outfielders are as important to winning a baseball game as any other players on the team. To be an outfielder you need eagle eyes, plenty of speed, sure fingers, and a strong arm. You also need good judgment so you will be able to decide what to do with the ball when you get it.

Very often, especially if your team's pitching is weak, the outfield is the busiest place on the diamond. So don't think that only unskilled rookies are sent there. An outfielder has to cover much more ground than an infielder. Because the outfield is a long way from the base-running action, an error there usually is more costly than an infield bobble.

Each outfielder has his own territory to guard. Yet there are no definite boundaries between center and right field or center and left. Fielders must help each other out. If the right fielder is chasing after a fly ball, and you in center field think you have a better chance to catch it, because you are moving toward the diamond or looking away from the sun, yell for it. "I got it! I got it!"

If you are the center fielder, you are expected to take charge of the outfield. You are in the best position to judge the play. Whenever there is any doubt who should field the ball, call out loud and clear. The fielder not making the catch must back up the play.

When in the outfield, you should watch every pitch. If possible, you should know the batting habits of the man at the plate. For a right-handed pull hitter, you should position yourself closer than usual toward the left-field foul line.

Pick the ball up with your eyes at the crack of the bat. By the sound of the contact you can tell pretty well whether it's going to be a high, looping fly ball or a fence buster. Your most valuable weapon is to get a

Race to where you figure the ball will be.

jump on the ball. Be moving before the echo from the bat dies out.

Make your estimate quickly and race to where you figure the ball will drop. By all means, if it's heading beyond you, turn and run. Don't back up. Get to the spot, then pivot toward the infield. Look up and locate the ball again. If possible, try to be moving forward toward the diamond when you catch it. Be able to judge how it will ricochet and play a hard-hit ball off the fence.

Of course, long before the ball is hit, you must plan what you will do with it if it comes your way. You know how many men are on base and on which bases. You have figured out what the runners will try to do. You remember how many outs there are. In other words, the whole game situation is laid out in your mind.

You try to catch a fly ball fairly high, with glove fingers pointed up. Avoid the basket catches. Few players can use them successfully. You also try to catch the ball near the shoulder of your throwing arm, cocking that arm back as the ball comes into your glove. Then pluck the ball from the glove with a simple, quick motion, stride forward a step, and throw a straight overhead bullet to a base or to the relay man.

You must always consider the direction of the wind and the effect it may have on a towering fly ball. Losing the ball in the sun is another hazard. Try to figure a way to catch the ball while facing at least partially away from its direct glare. Of course, sunglasses help.

Get in front of a ground ball. Like an infielder, the outfielder must keep his knees bent and the fingertips

Catch the fly ball at about eye level,
with glove fingers pointed up.

Get the ball back to the infield fast.

of his glove solidly on the ground. Don't spread your legs too wide. Any ball that gets through you or under your glove usually becomes a costly error. Some out-fielders get down on one knee to help block the ball.

116

Whether or not there are runners on base, never hold the ball after you catch it. Get it back to the infield as quickly as you can. With runners on base, throw hard and straight and low. The peg always should go ahead of the runner to keep him from advancing. Even if you have a cannon arm, don't try to reach home plate on the fly. Plan on getting your throw to the catcher on one or maybe even two bounces. Aim for the cutoff man's head, and he will have the chance to cut off the ball and make a relay throw if the play seems wise.

As an outfielder you should be in on every play, like any other player on the team. Rush in and back up throws to any base. Always be looking for a pick-off play. They are risky at best, so you want to be coming in to back up the baseman as soon as you see the pitcher make his move. Many an extra base and run have been avoided by such alertness on the part of out-fielders.

You may dream about those so-called circus catches when you tear in and dive for the ball, grabbing it on your shoestrings. As you go tumbling across the grass, arms and legs flying, you have about a fifty-fifty chance of holding on to the ball. If the catch means saving the game, by all means take any chance you need to in order to prevent a run from being scored. Even if you can't hold it, no one can blame you for trying. But there are times when the better play is to slow down and take the ball on a big bounce. In that way you can be sure of getting it back to the infield, rather than risk having it roll all the way to the fence.

These decisions require judgment. That's why an outfielder needs a head as good as his arm.

Since you usually have less work to do in the outfield than in the infield, you can put extra time and practice into your batting. In fact, most of the top hitters on any big-league team play the outfield. Often the fly chasers in the outfield are the players who wield a mean bat at the plate.

GAME WRAP-UP

There is a perfect way to make every play in baseball. There is a perfect place to lay down a bunt or hit the ball to get a runner around the bases. Supposedly there is also a perfect pitch to prevent the batter from doing so. A game can be played without hits, runs, or errors.

But who has ever played in one or even seen one? Not many to be sure, and that is how baseball should be. The game is action: throwing, hitting, running, catching, strike-outs, errors, and all.

You have heard the saying that baseball is a game of inches. True. One day you make a diving catch of an "impossible" line drive. You save the game. You are a hero. The next day the ball comes to you a scant inch farther away. It glances off your fingertips. The runner scores. You are a bum.

The difference is the real challenge of the game. Without errors, without strike-outs, baseball would be a dull game. The good ballplayer is the one who shakes off his boots and bobbles and practices harder to keep from making the same mistake again.

Sure, if you want to be a pitcher, you would like to have big hands, long arms, and long fingers. But don't let your physique scare you off. Your arm can be short and your fingers stubby, as long as you know how to pitch a ball. Not many people are born to be natural baseball players or natural anything else for that matter. Skills are acquired with lots of work and practice.

Of course, you'll be glad if you make a good play and overhear someone in the stands say, "Boy, that kid's got real talent!" But you know that talent is mostly hard work . . . and desire. You must keep wanting to play, even when things are tough. Baseball is a great and exciting game. Once you have played it, you usually are hooked.

Every coach, every player has his own favorite way to do something. As far as that person is concerned, since it works for him, it may be the *only* way. You may well improve your own game by giving his advice a try, especially if it is recommended by your coach. He has watched all kinds of players improve their hitting percentages by taking a different grip on the bat or by closing their stance a little at the plate. He can spot when you are not getting your glove low enough or dropping it soon enough to catch a hot grounder. Trying new things to correct old weaknesses is the best way to improve your game.

You don't need to follow every instruction to the letter. For instance, most pitchers will tell you to hold the ball along the seams so your index and middle fingers rest on plenty of stitches and give you firmer control. Fine. But a lot of the top pitchers grip the ball with their fingers across the seams and do just as well. Of course, their grip varies with the type of pitch that they are throwing.

In all phases of baseball there is plenty of room for variety and personal preference. The only real test of a technique is whether it is most comfortable for you. Do what works best for you.

Still, if you get into habits that vary too much from long-proven methods, your game will suffer. For instance, there is no way you can play your position properly or get hits unless you keep your eyes on the ball at all times. That is a cardinal rule, solid and invariable. You must be able to keep cool in the clutch. You cannot play good ball if you worry about your last error, grouse when something goes wrong, or blame the umpire when you strike out. You must keep loose and relaxed and eager.

You should, above all, have fun, for fun is what baseball is all about.

Baseball is a game of action and inches.

glossary

Balk—an illegal motion by the pitcher while trying to hold a runner on base.

Battery—the combination of pitcher and catcher.

Doubleheader—two games played in one day.

Ducks on the pond—runners on the bases.

Error—a fielder's fault to the runner's advantage.

Fair ball—a ball hit between the foul lines.

Force play—putting out a player who must leave his base because of other runners moving up behind.

Hook slide—sliding into base on a bent leg in order to avoid a tag.

Pine-tar rag—a sticky rag rubbed on bat or hands to improve grip. Similar to resin bag.

Pitchout—pitching wide of the batter in hopes that the catcher can peg out a base runner.

123

Pop-up—an easy fly ball to catch.

Pulling the ball—hitting to opposite field, as when a left-hander hits to right field or a right-hander to left.

Resin bag—a porous bag of powdered resin for dusting hands to aid the player's grip on ball or bat.

Rundown—a runner is caught, or "hung out," between bases and must try to escape a tag.

Southpaw—left-hander, or "port sider."

Squeeze play—a bunt laid down so a runner can score from third base.

Stance—the position a player takes in the batter's box.

Switch hitter—a batter who can hit either right- or left-handed.

Tag up—the runner stays on base until a fly ball is caught, then advances at his own risk.

Walk—a free base on balls when four pitches miss the strike zone.

index

* indicates illustration

125

126

Charles Coombs graduated from the University of California at Los Angeles and decided at once to make writing his career. Before he became an established writer he had jobs in clerking, carpentering, and aircraft building, working at his typewriter early in the morning and late at night. An athlete at school and college, Mr. Coombs began by writing sports fiction. He soon broadened his interests, writing adventure and mystery stories, and factual articles as well. When he had sold about a hundred stories he decided to try one year of full-time writing, chiefly for young people, and the results justified the decision. He now has published over a thousand stories and articles and many books, both fiction and nonfiction.

Mr. Coombs is married and has two sons and a daughter. His home is in Los Angeles.

Coombs, Charles Ira, 1914–
    Be a winner in baseball [by] Charles Coombs. Illustrated with 65 photos. and diagrs. New York, Morrow, 1973.

    127 p. illus. 22 cm. $4.25   4.25

    SUMMARY: Presents a brief history of baseball and instructs in improving the basic skills needed to play the game; sliding into base, fielding ground balls, making judgments, and many others.

    1. Baseball—Juvenile literature. [1. Baseball]   I. Title.

GV867.5.C66   796.357   72–7744
ISBN 0-688-20062-1 ; 0-688-30062-6 (lib. bdg.)   MARC